· TROPHIES ·

Spelling
Practice
Book

Grade 1

Harcourt

Orlando   Boston   Dallas   Chicago   San Diego

Visit *The Learning Site!*

www.harcourtschool.com

ISBN 0-15-323498-9

30   0982   17 16 15 14

4500470822

Level 1-4: Time Together

Level 1-5: Gather Around

© Harcourt

Name _____

► Write the letter or letters that complete each Spelling Word. Then trace the rest of the word. Use each word only once.

Spelling Words

1. ___ an

2. ___

3. m ___ d

4. ma ___

5. c ___ p

6. ca ___

7. ___ t

8. ___ at

at
hat
cat
can
cap
tap
map
mad
a
the

► Unscramble the letters to make a Spelling Word.

9. a t p
___

10. e h t
___

 SCHOOL-HOME CONNECTION Write the words *has, am, car,* and *man.* Have your child change one letter in each word to make a Spelling Word.

SPELLING PRACTICE BOOK
GUESS WHO • LESSON 1   5

© Harcourt

Word Sorts

▶ Make cards for the Spelling Words. Lay them down and read them.

1. Put the words with <u>a</u> in one group. Put the word without <u>a</u> in another group. Write the words on the chart.

Words With <u>a</u>	Word Without <u>a</u>

Spelling Words

at
hat
cat
can
cap
tap
map
mad
a
the
My Own Word

SCHOOL-HOME CONNECTION Have your child read each Spelling Word to you. Tell him or her to make a blue check mark next to all the words that have short *a* as in *am*, and a green check mark next to the words that do not have short *a*.

© Harcourt

Word Sorts

► Make cards for the Spelling Words. Lay them down and read them.

Spelling Words

am
ham
had
bad
bag
rag
cap
mad
up
go
My Own Word

1. Put the words with <u>a</u> in one group. Put the words without <u>a</u> in another group. Write the words on the chart.

2. Find the word with <u>u</u> and write it on the chart.

3. Find the word with <u>o</u> and write it on the chart.

Words With <u>a</u>	Words Without <u>a</u>
Word With <u>u</u>	**Word With <u>o</u>**

© Harcourt

SCHOOL-HOME CONNECTION Point to and read the Spelling Words aloud with your child. Talk about how the words are alike and how they are different.

SPELLING PRACTICE BOOK
GUESS WHO • LESSON 2   **7**

Name _____

▶ Write the letter or letters that complete each Spelling Word. Then trace the rest of the word. Use each word only once.

Spelling Words

am
ham
had
bad
bag
rag
cap
mad
up
go

1. r___g

2. ___p

3. ___ad

4. ___am

5. ___a___

6. h___d

7. m___d

8. ___o

▶ Unscramble the letters to make a Spelling Word.

9. p a c _____

10. a b g _____

SCHOOL-HOME CONNECTION Have your child read each Spelling Word to you. Ask him or her which words have short *a* as in *man*, short *u* as in *sun*, and which words have neither short *a* nor short *u*.

© Harcourt

Word Sorts

► Make cards for the Spelling Words. Lay them down and read them.

1. Put the words with i in one group. Put the words without i in another group. Write the words on the chart.

2. Put the words with a in one group. Put the words without a in another group. Write the words on the chart.

Spelling Words

| in |
| pin |
| pig |
| wig |
| win |
| fin |
| am |
| pan |
| yes |
| and |

My Own Word

Words With <u>i</u>	Words Without <u>i</u>
Words With <u>a</u>	**Words Without <u>a</u>**

SCHOOL-HOME CONNECTION Point to and read the Spelling Words aloud with your child. Talk about how the words are alike and how they are different.

SPELLING PRACTICE BOOK
GUESS WHO • LESSON 3   9

© Harcourt

Name _____

► Unscramble the letters to write a
   Spelling Word.

1. dna

_____

- - - - - - - - - - - - - -

_____

2. sey

_____

- - - - - - - - - - - - - -

_____

3. pni

_____

- - - - - - - - - - - - - -

_____

4. inw

_____

- - - - - - - - - - - - - -

_____

5. nfi

_____

- - - - - - - - - - - - - -

_____

6. anp

_____

- - - - - - - - - - - - - -

_____

7. ma

_____

- - - - - - - - - - - - - -

_____

8. igp

_____

- - - - - - - - - - - - - -

_____

9. giw

_____

- - - - - - - - - - - - - -

_____

10. ni

_____

- - - - - - - - - - - - - -

_____

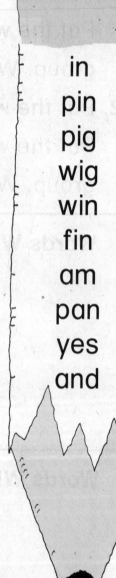

**Spelling
Words**

in
pin
pig
wig
win
fin
am
pan
yes
and

SCHOOL-HOME CONNECTION Have your child read
each Spelling Word to you. Talk about the vowel sound
you hear in each word.

© Harcourt

Name _____

Practice Test

Read each sentence. Look at how the two words are spelled. Fill in the oval next to the correct word.

SAMPLE: The _____ taps a ball.

⬜ kat   ⬛ cat

1. Mom has a _____.

⬜ bog   ⬜ bag

2. She has a _____ for Dad.

⬜ het   ⬜ hat

3. Did Mom win a _____?

⬜ wig   ⬜ wigg

4. _____, she did.

⬜ Yis   ⬜ Yes

5. Mom will be _____ to see me in the wig.

⬜ madd   ⬜ mad

Name _____

Practice Test

Read each pair of sentences. Look at how the underlined words are spelled. Then fill in the oval next to the correct sentence.

SAMPLE: ⬤ My class has a <u>map</u>.

◯ My class has a <u>mapp</u>.

1. ◯ A <u>pin</u> is in the map.

◯ A <u>pan</u> is in the map.

2. ◯ I <u>em</u> big.

◯ I <u>am</u> big.

3. ◯ I like to <u>go</u> here.

◯ I like to <u>goe</u> here.

4. ◯ I <u>can</u> walk home.

◯ I <u>kin</u> walk home.

5. ◯ I can hop <u>ap</u> and down.

◯ I can hop <u>up</u> and down.

© Harcourt

Name _____

Word Sorts

► Make cards for the Spelling Words.
Lay them down and read them.

1. Put the words with <u>a</u> in one group.
Put the words without <u>a</u> in another
group. Write the words on the chart.

2. Put the words with <u>i</u> in one group.
Put the words without <u>i</u> in another
group. Write the words on the chart.

Spelling Words

| pick |
| pack |
| tack |
| back |
| sack |
| sick |
| big |
| is |
| they |
| walk |
| My Own Word |

Words With <u>a</u>	Words Without <u>a</u>
Words With <u>i</u>	**Words Without <u>i</u>**

SCHOOL-HOME CONNECTION Point to and read the
Spelling Words aloud with your child. Talk about how the
words are alike and how they are different.

**SPELLING PRACTICE BOOK
GUESS WHO • LESSON 1** **13**

© Harcourt

Name _____

▶ Write the letter or letters that complete each Spelling Word. Then trace the rest of the word.

1. i __ __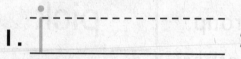

2. wal

3. the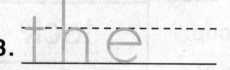

4. p a

5. s a k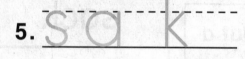

6. b i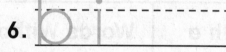

7. p __ ck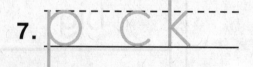

8. b a c

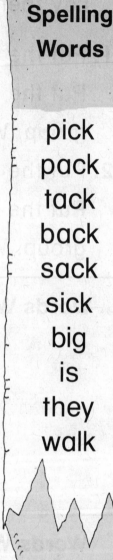

Spelling Words

pick
pack
tack
back
sack
sick
big
is
they
walk

▶ Unscramble the letters to make a Spelling Word.

9. k i s c

_____

10. k a t c

_____

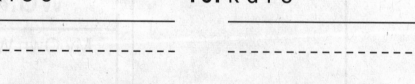

SCHOOL-HOME CONNECTION Write the words *park, wall, bag,* and *as:* Have your child change one letter in each word to make a Spelling Word.

© Harcourt

Name _____

▶ Unscramble the letters to write a
Spelling Word.

1. kacb

_____

- - - - - - - - - - -

_____

2. ont

_____

- - - - - - - - - - -

_____

3. tdo

_____

- - - - - - - - - - -

_____

4. opp

_____

- - - - - - - - - - -

_____

5. wtna

_____

- - - - - - - - - - -

_____

6. onw

_____

- - - - - - - - - - -

_____

7. otp

_____

- - - - - - - - - - -

_____

8. pho

_____

- - - - - - - - - - -

_____

9. tho

_____

- - - - - - - - - - -

_____

10. ipkc

_____

- - - - - - - - - - -

_____

Spelling Words

hot
hop
pop
pot
dot
not
back
pick
now
want

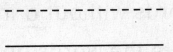
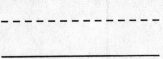
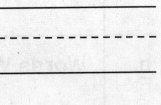

SCHOOL-HOME CONNECTION Have your child read
each Spelling Word to you. Ask her or him which words
have short *o* as in M*o*m, short *i* as in *it*, and which words
have neither short *o* nor short *i*.

© Harcourt

Name _____

Word Sorts

► Make cards for the Spelling Words.
Lay them down and read them.

1. Put the words with <u>o</u> in one group.
Put the words without <u>o</u> in another
group. Write the words on the chart.

2. Put the words with <u>a</u> in one group.
Put the words without <u>a</u> in another
group. Write the words on the chart.

Words With <u>o</u>	**Words Without <u>o</u>**
Words With <u>a</u>	**Words Without <u>a</u>**

Spelling Words

hot

hop

pop

pot

dot

not

back

pick

now

want

My Own Word

SCHOOL-HOME CONNECTION Point to and read the
Spelling Words aloud with your child. Talk about how
the words are alike and how they are different.

© Harcourt

Name _____

▶ Write the letter or letters that complete each Spelling Word. Then trace the rest of the word. Use each word only once.

Spelling Words

1. fa

2. o

3. ca

4. ta

5. n

6. al

7. b

8. f

all
call
fall
wall
ball
tall
on
not
so
of

▶ Unscramble the letters to make a Spelling Word.

9. a l w l

10. t n o

SCHOOL-HOME CONNECTION Have your child read each Spelling Word to you. Ask what letter pattern she or he notices in six of the words. Together, think of two more words that have the same letter pattern.

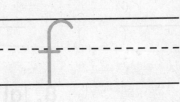

© Harcourt

Name _____

▶ Unscramble the letters to write a
Spelling Word.

1. latl

_____

- - - - - - - - -

_____

2. os

_____

- - - - - - - - -

_____

3. lafl

_____

- - - - - - - - -

_____

4. no

_____

- - - - - - - - -

_____

5. alcl

_____

- - - - - - - - -

_____

6. lalb

_____

- - - - - - - - -

_____

7. lwal

_____

- - - - - - - - -

_____

8. lal

_____

- - - - - - - - -

_____

9. fo

_____

- - - - - - - - -

_____

10. tno

_____

- - - - - - - - -

_____

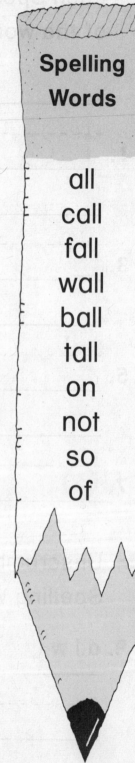

Spelling Words

all
call
fall
wall
ball
tall
on
not
so
of

SPELLING PRACTICE BOOK
GUESS WHO • LESSON 3

SCHOOL-HOME CONNECTION Point to and read the
Spelling Words aloud with your child. Talk about how
the words are alike and how they are different.

© Harcourt

Name _____

Practice Test

▶ Read each pair of sentences. Look at how the underlined words are spelled. Then fill in the oval next to the correct sentence.

SAMPLE: ⚬ Tom is not <u>bigg</u>.

━ Tom is not <u>big</u>.

1. ⚬ He is not <u>tal</u>.
   ⚬ He is not <u>tall</u>.

2. ⚬ Tom is on Dad's <u>back</u>.
   ⚬ Tom is on Dad's <u>bak</u>.

3. ⚬ <u>Now</u> Tom is tall!
   ⚬ <u>No</u> Tom is tall!

4. ⚬ His ball looks like a <u>dat</u>.
   ⚬ His ball looks like a <u>dot</u>.

5. ⚬ Tom will <u>not</u> come down!
   ⚬ Tom will <u>nott</u> come down!

Name _____

Practice Test

▶ Read each sentence. Look at how the two words are spelled. Fill in the oval next to the correct word.

SAMPLE: Jim has a big _____ .

   ● sack   ⊂⊃ sak

1. They _____ balls in the sack.

   ⊂⊃ pack   ⊂⊃ pak

2. The balls _____ down!

   ⊂⊃ fal   ⊂⊃ fall

3. Dad tells Jim to _____ up the balls.

   ⊂⊃ pic   ⊂⊃ pick

4. Jim asks if _____ can play.

   ⊂⊃ they   ⊂⊃ thay

5. Dad will _____ to play!

   ⊂⊃ want   ⊂⊃ won

© Harcourt

Name _____

▶ Unscramble the letters to write a
Spelling Word.

**Spelling
Words**

hen
pen
men
end
send
set
all
call
very
that

1. nep

_____

- - - - - - - - - - - -

_____

2. htta

_____

- - - - - - - - - - - -

_____

3. lal

_____

- - - - - - - - - - - -

_____

4. ndse

_____

- - - - - - - - - - - -

_____

5. enm

_____

- - - - - - - - - - - -

_____

6. yerv

_____

- - - - - - - - - - - -

_____

7. ned

_____

- - - - - - - - - - - -

_____

8. lacl

_____

- - - - - - - - - - - -

_____

9. tse

_____

- - - - - - - - - - - -

_____

10. hne

_____

- - - - - - - - - - - -

_____

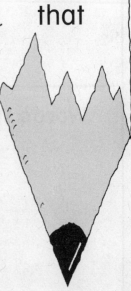

© Harcourt

SCHOOL-HOME CONNECTION Have your child read
each Spelling Word to you. Then ask which words have the
short *e* sound as in *egg*.

Word Sorts

▶ Make cards for the Spelling Words. Lay them down and read them.

1. Put the words with <u>e</u> in one group. Put the words without <u>e</u> in another group. Write the words on the chart.

2. Put the words with <u>a</u> in one group. Put the words without <u>a</u> in another group. Write the words on the chart.

Words With <u>e</u>	Words Without <u>e</u>
Words With <u>a</u>	**Words Without <u>a</u>**

Spelling Words

hen

pen

men

end

send

set

all

call

very

that

My Own Word

© Harcourt

SCHOOL-HOME CONNECTION Point to and read the Spelling Words aloud with your child. Talk about how the words are alike and how they are different.

Word Sorts

Spelling Words

▶ Make cards for the Spelling Words.
Lay them down and read them.

1. Put the words with <u>th</u> in one group.
Put the words without <u>th</u> in another
group. Write the words on the chart.

2. Put the words with <u>e</u> in one group.
Put the words with <u>a</u> in another
group. Write the words on the chart.

Words With <u>th</u>	Words Without <u>th</u>
Words With <u>e</u>	**Words With <u>a</u>**

Spelling Words
then
them
this
that
path
with
men
set
was
said
My Own Word

SCHOOL-HOME CONNECTION Point to and read the
Spelling Words aloud with your child. Talk about how the
words are alike and how they are different.

SPELLING PRACTICE BOOK
CATCH A DREAM • LESSON 2   **23**

© Harcourt

Name _____

▶ Write the letter or letters that complete each Spelling Word. Then trace the rest of the word.

Spelling Words

then
them
this
that
path
with
men
set
was
said

1. _w a___

2. _t e n___

3. _p t h___

4. _s d___

5. _t a t___

6. _i s___

7. _e m___

8. _s e___

▶ Unscramble the letters to make a Spelling Word.

9. e m n

_____

10. h i t w

_____

SCHOOL-HOME CONNECTION Write the words *thin*, *man*, *sat*, and *than*. Have your child change one letter in each word to make a Spelling Word.

© Harcourt

▶ Unscramble the letters to write a
Spelling Word.

1. gru

_____

- - - - - - - - - - - -

_____

2. neth

_____

- - - - - - - - - - - -

_____

3. stmu

_____

- - - - - - - - - - - -

_____

4. gub

_____

- - - - - - - - - - - -

_____

5. su

_____

- - - - - - - - - - - -

_____

6. tihw

_____

- - - - - - - - - - - -

_____

7. eus

_____

- - - - - - - - - - - -

_____

8. hes

_____

- - - - - - - - - - - -

_____

9. ubs

_____

- - - - - - - - - - - -

_____

10. ugm

_____

- - - - - - - - - - - -

_____

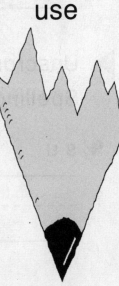

**Spelling
Words**

us
bus
bug
rug
mug
must
with
then
she
use

SCHOOL-HOME CONNECTION Have your child read
each Spelling Word to you. Ask him or her to say the
words that have the short *u* sound as in *up*.

SPELLING PRACTICE BOOK
CATCH A DREAM • LESSON 3   25

© Harcourt

Name _____

▶ Write the letter or letters that complete each Spelling Word. Then trace the rest of the word. Use each word only once.

1.  b g

2. 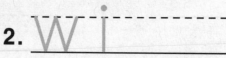 w i

3. 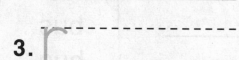 r

4. 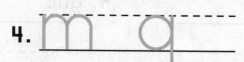 m g

5. 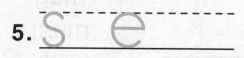 s   e

6. 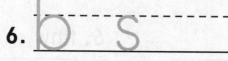 b   s

7.    s e

8.  t e n

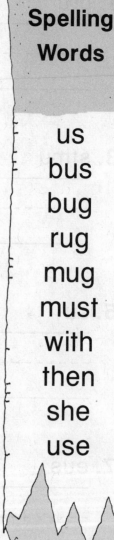

Spelling Words

us
bus
bug
rug
mug
must
with
then
she
use

▶ Unscramble the letters to make a Spelling Word.

9. s u

_____

10. t s m u

_____

SPELLING PRACTICE BOOK
CATCH A DREAM • LESSON 3

SCHOOL-HOME CONNECTION Write the words *mush*, *them*, *but*, and *is*. Have your child change one letter in each word to make a Spelling Word.

© Harcourt

▶ Unscramble the letters to write a
Spelling Word.

1. rouy

_____

- - - - - - - - - - -

_____

2. agnr

_____

- - - - - - - - - - -

_____

**Spelling
Words**

3. gans

_____

- - - - - - - - - - -

_____

4. bsu

_____

- - - - - - - - - - -

_____

5. stum

_____

- - - - - - - - - - -

_____

6. irgn

_____

- - - - - - - - - - -

_____

sing
sang
hang
rang
ring
bring
bus
must
your
when

7. enhw

_____

- - - - - - - - - - -

_____

8. isgn

_____

- - - - - - - - - - -

_____

9. gahn

_____

- - - - - - - - - - -

_____

10. nibrg

_____

- - - - - - - - - - -

_____

SCHOOL-HOME CONNECTION Have your child read
each Spelling Word to you. Tell him or her to make a
check mark next to all the words that have *ng* as in *thing*.

© Harcourt

Name _____

▶ Write the letter or letters that complete each Spelling Word. Then trace the rest of the word. Use each word only once.

Spelling Words

sing
sang
hang
rang
ring
bring
bus
must
your
when

1. _ang

2. bri_

3. w_en

4. ra_

5. rin_

6. bu_

7. m_st

8. si_g

▶ Unscramble the letters to make a Spelling Word.

9. r u y o

_____

10. n h g a

_____

SPELLING PRACTICE BOOK
CATCH A DREAM • LESSON 4

SCHOOL-HOME CONNECTION Write the words *but*, *hand*, and *four*. Have your child change one letter in each word to make a Spelling Word.

© Harcourt

Word Sorts

▶ Make cards for the Spelling Words.
Lay them down and read them.

1. Put the words with <u>or</u> in one group.
Put the words without <u>or</u> in another
group. Write the words on the chart.

2. Put the words with <u>ng</u> in one group.
Put the words without <u>ng</u> in another
group. Write the words on the chart.

Spelling Words

or
for
corn
cork
fork
more
hang
ring
two
from

My Own Word

Words With <u>or</u>	Words Without <u>or</u>
Words With <u>ng</u>	**Words Without <u>ng</u>**

SCHOOL-HOME CONNECTION Shuffle the Spelling
Word cards, then point to each one and have your child
read it to you. Talk about how the words are alike and
how they are different.

SPELLING PRACTICE BOOK
CATCH A DREAM • LESSON 5   29

© Harcourt

Name _____

▶ Write the letter or letters that complete each Spelling Word. Then trace the rest of the word.

Spelling Words

or
for
corn
cork
fork
more
hang
ring
two
from

1.  mor

2. 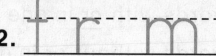 f r m

3.  o

4. 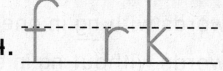 f rk

5. t

6.  r i n

7. 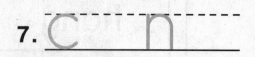 c n

8. 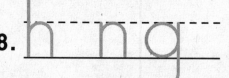 h ng

▶ Unscramble the letters to make a Spelling Word.

9. o f r _____

10. r o c k _____

SCHOOL-HOME CONNECTION Ask your child to name the Spelling Words that rhyme.

© Harcourt

Name _____

► Unscramble the letters to write a
   Spelling Word.

1. psih
_____

- - - - - - - - - - -

_____

2. hisw
_____

- - - - - - - - - - -

3. eb
_____

- - - - - - - - - - -

_____

4. ermo
_____

- - - - - - - - - - -

5. shad
_____

- - - - - - - - - - -

_____

6. oths
_____

- - - - - - - - - - -

7. hops
_____

- - - - - - - - - - -

8. ryt
_____

- - - - - - - - - - -

9. dhsi
_____

- - - - - - - - - - -

10. rof
_____

- - - - - - - - - - -

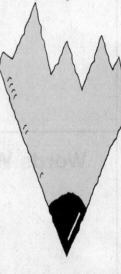

**Spelling
Words**

ship
shop
shot
wish
dish
dash
for
more
be
try

SCHOOL-HOME CONNECTION Have your child read
each Spelling Word to you. Tell him or her to circle all
the words that have *sh* as in *fish* or *short*.

SPELLING PRACTICE BOOK
CATCH A DREAM • LESSON 6   **31**

© Harcourt

Word Sorts

▶ Make cards for the Spelling Words.
Lay them down and read them.

1. Put the words with <u>sh</u> in one group
and without <u>sh</u> in another group.
Write the words on the chart.

2. Group the words with <u>or</u> and write
them on the chart.

3. Put the words without <u>sh</u> or <u>or</u> in a
group, and write them on the chart.

Spelling Words

| ship |
| shop |
| shot |
| wish |
| dish |
| dash |
| for |
| more |
| be |
| try |
| My Own Word |

Words With <u>sh</u>	Words Without <u>sh</u>
Words With <u>or</u>	**Words Without sh or or**

SCHOOL-HOME CONNECTION Ask your child why she or he wrote the Spelling Words where they appear on the chart.

© Harcourt

Name _____

Practice Test

► Read each sentence. Look at how the two words are spelled. Fill in the oval next to the correct word.

SAMPLE: A _____ and a cat met on a path.

   ━ hen   ◯ henn

1. The hen wanted _____ .
   ◯ coren   ◯ corn

2. The cat _____ it was all gone.
   ◯ said   ◯ sed

3. "You _____ help me!" cried the hen.
   ◯ must   ◯ musst

4. "I _____ I could help," sniffed the cat.
   ◯ wis   ◯ wish

5. "I am _____ sad for you," added the cat.
   ◯ very   ◯ varey

Name _____

Practice Test

▶ Read each pair of sentences. Look at how the underlined words are spelled. Then fill in the oval next to the correct sentence.

SAMPLE: ⬭ Jim likes to <u>singe</u> all day.

⬭ Jim likes to <u>sing</u> all day.

1. ⬭ He sings on the <u>bus</u>.
   ⬭ He sings on the <u>bug</u>.

2. ⬭ He sings when we <u>ship</u>.
   ⬭ He sings when we <u>shop</u>.

3. ⬭ <u>Wen</u> he walks, he sings.
   ⬭ <u>When</u> he walks, he sings.

4. ⬭ Friends <u>call</u> and ask him to sing.
   ⬭ Friends <u>coll</u> and ask him to sing.

5. ⬭ Jim will not <u>heng</u> up on them.
   ⬭ Jim will not <u>hang</u> up on them.

© Harcourt

Name _____

Word Sorts

Spelling Words

► Make cards for the Spelling Words.
Lay them down and read them.

1. Put the words with <u>ch</u> in one group
   and without <u>ch</u> in another group.
   Write the words on the chart.

2. Put the words with <u>sh</u> in a group,
   and write them on the chart.

3. Put the words with <u>a</u> in a group,
   and write them on the chart.

Words With <u>ch</u>	Words Without <u>ch</u>
Words With <u>sh</u>	**Words With <u>a</u>**

Spelling Words
chip
chin
inch
itch
catch
match
wish
shop
how
many
My Own Word

SCHOOL-HOME CONNECTION Shuffle the Spelling
Word cards. Then point to each one and have your child
read it aloud. Talk about how the words are alike and how
they are different.

© Harcourt

▶ Write the letter or letters that complete each Spelling Word. Then trace the rest of the word.

Spelling Words

chip
chin
inch
itch
catch
match
wish
shop
how
many

1.  h   w

2.  mat h

3. 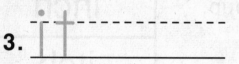 it

4. 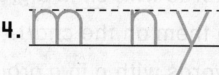 m ny

5.  op

6.  in

7. 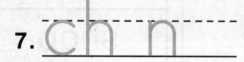 ch n

8.  ca ch

▶ Unscramble the letters to make a Spelling Word.

9. h s w i

_____

10. p i c h

_____

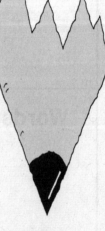

SCHOOL-HOME CONNECTION Write the words *hatch, cow, ship,* and *wash*. Have your child change one letter in each word to make a Spelling Word.

© Harcourt

Name _____

► Unscramble the letters to write a
Spelling Word.

Spelling Words

1. noso
_____
- - - - - - - - -
_____

2. rma
_____
- - - - - - - - -
_____

3. arf
_____
- - - - - - - - -
_____

4. rcad
_____
- - - - - - - - -
_____

5. ichn
_____
- - - - - - - - -
_____

6. elvi
_____
- - - - - - - - -
_____

7. tra
_____
- - - - - - - - -
_____

8. mrfa
_____
- - - - - - - - -
_____

9. cinh
_____
- - - - - - - - -
_____

10. crta
_____
- - - - - - - - -
_____

far
farm
arm
art
cart
card
chin
inch
live
soon

© Harcourt

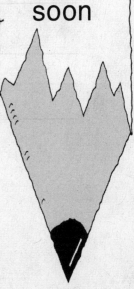

SCHOOL-HOME CONNECTION Have your child read
each Spelling Word to you. Tell him or her to spell three
favorite words from the list.

Name _____

▶ Write the letter or letters that complete each Spelling Word. Then trace the rest of the word.

Spelling Words

far
farm
arm
art
cart
card
chin
inch
live
soon

1. ___ m

2. ca t

3. li ___

4. i ch

5. ___ ar

6. ch ___

7. s ___ n

8. ___ a t

9. ___ ard

10. fa m

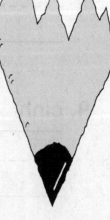

SCHOOL-HOME CONNECTION Write the words *form*, *chip*, and *fur*. Have your child change one letter in each word to make a Spelling Word.

© Harcourt

Name _____

▶ Unscramble the letters to write a
Spelling Word.

1. uqcik

_____

_____

2. radc

_____

_____

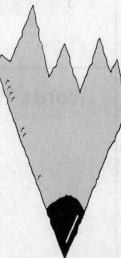

**Spelling
Words**

quit
quick
quiz
whiz
which
when
arm
card
who
there

3. owh

_____

_____

4. mar

_____

_____

5. teerh

_____

_____

6. ciwhh

_____

_____

7. zuqi

_____

_____

8. enhw

_____

_____

9. tiqu

_____

_____

10. wzhi

_____

_____

© Harcourt

SCHOOL-HOME CONNECTION Have your child read
each Spelling Word to you. Ask him or her to spell three
favorite words from the list.

Word Sorts

► Make cards for the Spelling Words.
Lay them down and read them.

Spelling Words

| quit |
| quick |
| quiz |
| whiz |
| which |
| when |
| arm |
| card |
| who |
| there |

My Own Word

1. Put the words with <u>wh</u> in one group
and without <u>wh</u> in another group.
Write the words on the chart.

2. Put the words with <u>qu</u> in one group
and without <u>qu</u> in another group.
Write the words on the chart.

Words With <u>wh</u>	Words Without <u>wh</u>

Words With <u>qu</u>	Words Without <u>qu</u>

SCHOOL-HOME CONNECTION Point to and read the
Spelling Words aloud with your child. Talk about how
the words are alike and how they are different.

© Harcourt

Word Sorts

► Make cards for the Spelling Words.
Lay them down and read them.

1. Put the words with <u>ir</u> in one group.
Then write the words on the chart.

2. Put the words with <u>ur</u> in one group.
Then write the words on the chart.

3. Find the word with <u>er</u> and write it on
the chart.

4. Find the word with <u>or</u> and write it on
the chart.

Spelling Words

sir
dirt
bird
burn
fur
her
quit
when
work
grew
My Own Word

Words With <u>ir</u>	Words With <u>ur</u>
Word With <u>er</u>	**Word With <u>or</u>**

© Harcourt

SCHOOL-HOME CONNECTION Talk to your child
about the letters that stand for the vowel sound in
each Spelling Word.

SPELLING PRACTICE BOOK
HERE AND THERE • LESSON 4   **41**

Name _____

▶ Write the letter or letters that complete
each Spelling Word. Then trace the rest
of the word.

Spelling Words

sir
dirt
bird
burn
fur
her
quit
when
work
grew

1.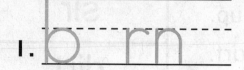

2.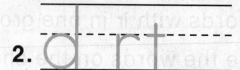

3.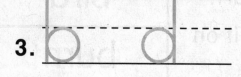

4.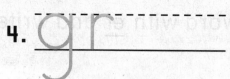

5.

6.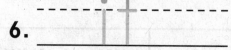

7.

8.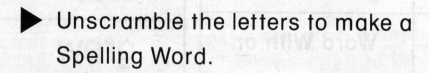

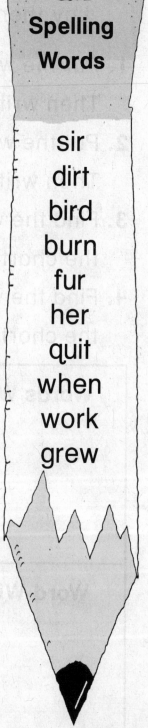

▶ Unscramble the letters to make a
Spelling Word.

9. n w h e

_____

10. u r f

_____

SCHOOL-HOME CONNECTION Write the words drew,
barn, word, and then. Have your child change one letter
in each word to make a Spelling Word.

© Harcourt

Name _____

► Unscramble the letters to write a
  Spelling Word.

1. lieggg

_____
- - - - - - - - - - - -
_____

2. idfled

_____
- - - - - - - - - - - -
_____

3. dluced

_____
- - - - - - - - - - - -
_____

4. ufr

_____
- - - - - - - - - - - -
_____

5. drib

_____
- - - - - - - - - - - -
_____

6. wlgige

_____
- - - - - - - - - - - -
_____

7. dideml

_____
- - - - - - - - - - - -
_____

8. eerw

_____
- - - - - - - - - - - -
_____

9. eldpud

_____
- - - - - - - - - - - -
_____

10. rofu

_____
- - - - - - - - - - - -
_____

**Spelling
Words**

middle
fiddle
wiggle
giggle
puddle
cuddle
fur
bird
were
four

© Harcourt

SCHOOL-HOME CONNECTION Have your child read
each Spelling Word to you. Tell him or her to make a star
next to the words that end in *le*.

**SPELLING PRACTICE BOOK
HERE AND THERE • LESSON 5**   **43**

Name _____

▶ Complete each Spelling Word.

1. gig_____

2. __ird

3. cu____

4. f__r

5. m__ddle

6. __re

7. pud____

8. f__r

9. wi____

10. fi__le

**Spelling
Words**

middle
fiddle
wiggle
giggle
puddle
cuddle
fur
bird
were
four

SCHOOL-HOME CONNECTION Write the words
goggle, wore, for, and *muddle.* Have your child change one
letter in each word to make a Spelling Word.

© Harcourt

Name _____

▶ Unscramble the letters to write a Spelling Word.

1. wro
_____
- - - - - - - - - - - -
_____

2. posa
_____
- - - - - - - - - - - -
_____

3. cohols
_____
- - - - - - - - - - - -
_____

4. gliweg
_____
- - - - - - - - - - - -
_____

5. owl
_____
- - - - - - - - - - - -
_____

6. tabo
_____
- - - - - - - - - - - -
_____

7. dimeld
_____
- - - - - - - - - - - -
_____

8. klat
_____
- - - - - - - - - - - -

9. drao
_____
- - - - - - - - - - - -
_____

10. wob
_____
- - - - - - - - - - - -

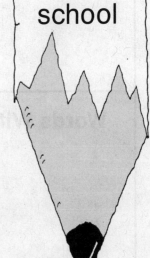

Spelling Words

low
bow
row
road
soap
boat
wiggle
middle
talk
school

© Harcourt

SCHOOL-HOME CONNECTION Have your child read each Spelling Word to you. Ask which words have long *o* as in *coat* and which have long *o* as in *tow*.

Word Sorts

► Make cards for the Spelling Words.
Lay them down and read them.

1. Put the words with <u>ow</u> in one group.
Put the words without <u>ow</u> in another
group. Write the words on the chart.

2. Put the words with <u>oa</u> in one group.
Put the words without <u>oa</u> in another
group. Write the words on the chart.

Words With <u>ow</u>	Words Without <u>ow</u>
Words With <u>oa</u>	**Words Without <u>oa</u>**

Spelling Words

low
bow
row
road
soap
boat
wiggle
middle
talk
school
My Own Word

SCHOOL-HOME CONNECTION Shuffle the Spelling
Word cards, and have your child read them aloud.

© Harcourt

Practice Test

▶ Read each sentence. Look at how the two words are spelled. Fill in the oval next to the correct word.

SAMPLE: Sal lives on a _____.

● farm   ⬭ ferm

1. She _____ up on that farm.
   ⬭ grue   ⬭ grew

2. She has a lot of animals _____.
   ⬭ there   ⬭ thair

3. She must _____ hard.
   ⬭ work   ⬭ wirk

4. She will not _____.
   ⬭ quit   ⬭ quitt

5. She has _____ fun pets.
   ⬭ meny   ⬭ many

Name _____

Practice Test

▶ Read each pair of sentences. Look at how the underlined words are spelled. Then fill in the oval next to the correct sentence.

SAMPLE: ⬭ I wish I <u>werr</u> a pig.

➖ I wish I <u>were</u> a pig.

1. ⬭ A pig can go in a <u>puddle</u>.
   ⬭ A pig can go in a <u>puddal</u>.

2. ⬭ I want to fly like a <u>berd</u>.
   ⬭ I want to fly like a <u>bird</u>.

3. ⬭ A dog can walk on the <u>rowd</u>.
   ⬭ A dog can walk on the <u>road</u>.

4. ⬭ I could be in a <u>school</u> of fish.
   ⬭ I could be in a <u>skool</u> of fish.

5. ⬭ Could I <u>liv</u> on a farm?
   ⬭ Could I <u>live</u> on a farm?

© Harcourt

Word Sorts

▶ Make cards for the Spelling Words.
Lay them down and read them.

1. Put the words with long <u>e</u> in one
group and without long <u>e</u> in another.
Write the words on the chart.

2. Put the words with long <u>o</u> in one
group and without long <u>o</u> in another.
Write the words on the chart.

Spelling Words

| me |
| mean |
| bean |
| be |
| beet |
| feet |
| low |
| road |
| who |
| door |
| My Own Word |

Words With Long <u>e</u>	Words Without Long <u>e</u>
Words With Long <u>o</u>	**Words Without Long <u>o</u>**

SCHOOL-HOME CONNECTION Shuffle the Spelling
Word cards. Talk about how the words are alike and how
they are different.

SPELLING PRACTICE BOOK
TIME TOGETHER • LESSON 1   49

© Harcourt

Name _____

► Write the letter or letters that complete
each Spelling Word. Then trace the rest
of the word.

1.

2.

3.

4.

5.

6.

7.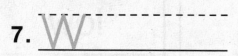

8.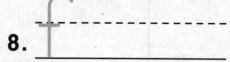

Spelling Words

me
mean
bean
be
beet
feet
low
road
who
door

► Unscramble the letters to make a
Spelling Word.

9. a r o d
_____

10. o r d o
_____

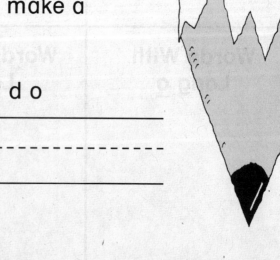

SCHOOL-HOME CONNECTION Write the words *bow*,
poor, *beam*, and *we*. Have your child change one letter in
each word to make a Spelling Word.

© Harcourt

► Unscramble the letters to write a Spelling Word.

1. etla

_____

_ _ _ _ _ _ _ _ _ _

_____

2. tefe

_____

_ _ _ _ _ _ _ _ _ _

3. em

_____

_ _ _ _ _ _ _ _ _ _

4. kown

_____

_ _ _ _ _ _ _ _ _ _

5. acme

_____

_ _ _ _ _ _ _ _ _ _

_____

6. loas

_____

_ _ _ _ _ _ _ _ _ _

7. elka

_____

_ _ _ _ _ _ _ _ _ _

_____

8. meag

_____

_ _ _ _ _ _ _ _ _ _

_____

9. keta

_____

_ _ _ _ _ _ _ _ _ _

_____

10. aegt

_____

_ _ _ _ _ _ _ _ _ _

_____

Spelling Words

came
game
gate
late
lake
take
feet
me
know
also

SCHOOL-HOME CONNECTION Have your child read each Spelling Word to you. Ask him or her to name the Spelling Words with long *a*, with long *o*, and with long *e*.

© Harcourt

Name _____

▶ Write the letter or letters that complete each Spelling Word. Then trace the rest of the word.

Spelling Words

came
game
gate
late
lake
take
feet
me
know
also

1. _e_

2. _gat_

3. _al_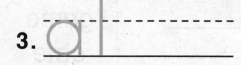

4. _t_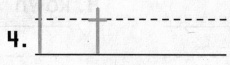

5. _g m_

6. _now_

7. _t k_

8. _c_

▶ Unscramble the letters to make a Spelling Word.

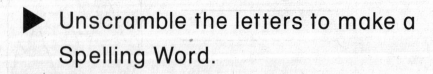

9. e l a k
_____

10. e f e t
_____

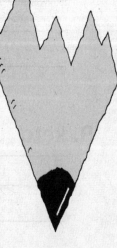

SCHOOL-HOME CONNECTION Write the words *tame, knot, mate,* and *feel.* Have your child change one letter in each word to make a Spelling Word.

© Harcourt

Name _____

▶ Unscramble the letters to write a
Spelling Word.

**Spelling
Words**

1. leybl
_____
- - - - - - - - - - - - - -
_____

2. lodwr
_____
- - - - - - - - - - - - - -
_____

3. vero
_____
- - - - - - - - - - - - - -
_____

4. yruhr
_____
- - - - - - - - - - - - - -
_____

5. lejly
_____
- - - - - - - - - - - - - -
_____

6. fynun
_____
- - - - - - - - - - - - - -
_____

7. ecam
_____
- - - - - - - - - - - - - -
_____

8. nnbyu
_____
- - - - - - - - - - - - - -
_____

9. yurfr
_____
- - - - - - - - - - - - - -
_____

10. kaet
_____
- - - - - - - - - - - - - -
_____

jelly
belly
bunny
funny
furry
hurry
take
came
world
over

© Harcourt

SCHOOL-HOME CONNECTION Have your child read
each Spelling Word to you. Ask what is the same about
the first six words in the list.

SPELLING PRACTICE BOOK
TIME TOGETHER • LESSON 3   53

Word Sorts

▶ Make cards for the Spelling Words.
Lay them on your desk and read them.

1. Put the words that end with y in one
group and the words without y in
another group. Write the words on
the chart.

2. Put the words with long a in one group
and those without long a in another
group. Write the words on the chart.

Words With y	Words Without y
Words With Long a	**Words Without Long a**

Spelling Words

jelly
belly
bunny
funny
furry
hurry
take
came
world
over
My Own Word

© Harcourt

SCHOOL-HOME CONNECTION Point to and read the
Spelling Words aloud with your child. Talk about how
the words are alike and how they are different.

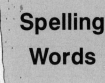

▶ Unscramble the letters to write a
Spelling Word.

1. enni

_____

- - - - - - - - - - - - -

_____

2. teib

_____

- - - - - - - - - - - - -

_____

3. lkie

_____

- - - - - - - - - - - - -

_____

4. rawm

_____

- - - - - - - - - - - - -

_____

5. yhrur

_____

- - - - - - - - - - - - -

_____

6. traew

_____

- - - - - - - - - - - - -

_____

7. elni

_____

- - - - - - - - - - - - -

_____

8. kibe

_____

- - - - - - - - - - - - -

_____

9. hiwle

_____

- - - - - - - - - - - - -

_____

10. nufny

_____

- - - - - - - - - - - - -

_____

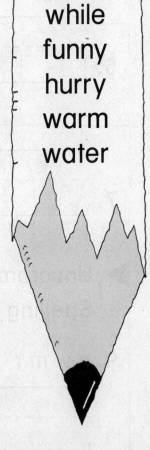

**Spelling
Words**

nine
line
like
bike
bite
while
funny
hurry
warm
water

© Harcourt

SCHOOL-HOME CONNECTION Have your child read
each Spelling Word to you. Ask him or her what vowel
sound is in each word, and what letters stand for the
sound in the word.

Name _____

▶ Write the letter or letters that complete each Spelling Word. Then trace the rest of the word.

Spelling Words

nine
line
like
bike
bite
while
funny
hurry
warm
water

1. li k

2. wh

3. hu

4. bik

5. n n

6. fun

7. wat

8. lin

▶ Unscramble the letters to make a Spelling Word.

9. a w m r

_____

10. e b t i

_____

SCHOOL-HOME CONNECTION Write the words *fine,* *life,* and *sunny.* Have your child change one letter in each word to make a Spelling Word.

© Harcourt

▶ Unscramble the letters to write a
Spelling Word.

1. peacs

_____

- - - - - - - - - - - - -

_____

2. ilke

_____

- - - - - - - - - - - - -

_____

3. stom

_____

- - - - - - - - - - - - -

_____

4. eic

_____

- - - - - - - - - - - - -

_____

5. acre

_____

- - - - - - - - - - - - -

_____

6. hyw

_____

- - - - - - - - - - - - -

_____

7. cafe

_____

- - - - - - - - - - - - -

_____

8. ecin

_____

- - - - - - - - - - - - -

_____

9. ceir

_____

- - - - - - - - - - - - -

_____

10. ienn

_____

- - - - - - - - - - - - -

_____

**Spelling
Words**

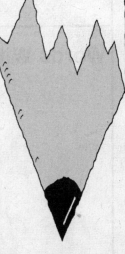

ice
nice
rice
race
face
space
like
nine
why
most

© Harcourt

SCHOOL-HOME CONNECTION Have your child read
each Spelling Word aloud to you. Ask what he or she has
learned about the letter *c*.

Word Sorts

▶ Make cards for the Spelling Words.
Lay them down and read them.

1. Put the words with long i in one group
   and those without long i in another
   group. Write the words on the chart.

2. Put the words with long a in one group
   and those without long a in another
   group. Write the words on the chart.

Words With Long i	Words Without Long i
Words With Long a	**Words Without Long a**

Spelling Words

ice
nice
rice
race
face
space
like
nine
why
most
My Own Word

SCHOOL-HOME CONNECTION Shuffle the Spelling Word Cards, then point to each one and read it aloud with your child. Talk about how the words are alike and how they are different.

© Harcourt

Word Sorts

► Make cards for the Spelling Words.
Lay them down and read them.

1. Put the words with <u>ow</u> in one group
   and those without <u>ow</u> in another
   group. Write the words on the chart.

2. Put the words with <u>ou</u> in one group
   and those without <u>ou</u> in another
   group. Write the words on the chart.

Words With <u>ow</u>	Words Without <u>ow</u>
Words With <u>ou</u>	**Words Without <u>ou</u>**

Spelling Words

cow

how

now

down

out

round

nice

face

does

once

My Own Word

© Harcourt

SCHOOL-HOME CONNECTION Shuffle the Spelling
Word cards. Point to each one and have your child read it
aloud. Talk about how the words are alike and how they
are different.

Name _____

► Write the letter or letters that complete
each Spelling Word. Then trace the rest
of the word.

**Spelling
Words**

1. 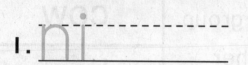 2.

3.  4.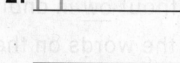

cow
how
now
down
out
round
nice
face
does
once

5. 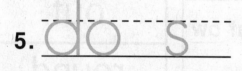 6.

7. 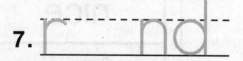 8.

► Unscramble the letters to make a
Spelling Word.

9. e f c a 10. w o n d

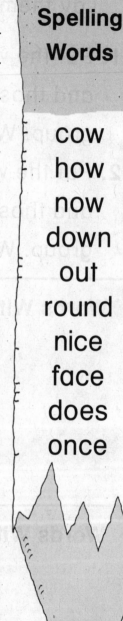

 SCHOOL-HOME CONNECTION Write the words *found,
mice, town,* and *our.* Have your child change one letter in
each word to make a Spelling Word.

© Harcourt

Name _____

► Unscramble the letters to write a
   Spelling Word.

1. onw

_____

- - - - - - - - - - - - - -

_____

2. syk

_____

- - - - - - - - - - - - - -

_____

3. gihet

_____

- - - - - - - - - - - - - -

_____

4. tuo

_____

- - - - - - - - - - - - - -

_____

5. ym

_____

- - - - - - - - - - - - - -

_____

6. yan

_____

- - - - - - - - - - - - - -

_____

7. ylf

_____

- - - - - - - - - - - - - -

_____

8. hyw

_____

- - - - - - - - - - - - - -

_____

9. tyr

_____

- - - - - - - - - - - - - -

_____

10. yb

_____

- - - - - - - - - - - - - -

_____

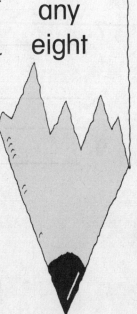

Spelling Words

my
fly
by
why
sky
try
out
now
any
eight

© Harcourt

SCHOOL-HOME CONNECTION Have your child read
each Spelling Word to you. Talk about the rhyming words
on the list.

Name _____

▶ Write the letter or letters that complete each Spelling Word. Then trace the rest of the word.

Spelling Words

1. w___y

2. ___y

3. b___

4. ___ny

5. ei___ht

6. o___t

7. no___

8. ___ly

9. ___t

10. s___

my
fly
by
why
sky
try
out
now
any
eight

SCHOOL-HOME CONNECTION Write the words *and, be, not,* and *night.* Have your child change one letter in each word to make a Spelling Word.

© Harcourt

Name _____

▶ Unscramble the letters to write a Spelling Word.

1. ulbe

_____

– – – – – – – –

_____

2. neco

_____

– – – – – – – –

_____

3. hoste

_____

– – – – – – – –

_____

4. ym

_____

– – – – – – – –

_____

5. deoc

_____

– – – – – – – –

_____

6. nagia

_____

– – – – – – – –

_____

7. dore

_____

– – – – – – – –

_____

8. beno

_____

– – – – – – – –

_____

9. osre

_____

– – – – – – – –

_____

10. tyr

_____

– – – – – – – –

_____

**Spelling
Words**

bone
cone
code
rode
rose
those
my
try
again
blue

© Harcourt

SCHOOL-HOME CONNECTION Have your child read each Spelling Word to you. Tell him or her to name pairs of Spelling Words that rhyme.

Name _____

Word Sorts

Spelling Words

► Make cards for the Spelling Words.
Lay them down and read them.

1. Put the words with long <u>o</u> in one
   group and those without long <u>o</u> in
   another. Write the words on the chart.

2. Put the words with <u>y</u> in one group
   and those without <u>y</u> in another.
   Write the words on the chart.

| bone |
| cone |
| code |
| rode |
| rose |
| those |
| my |
| try |
| again |
| blue |
| My Own Word |

Words With Long <u>o</u>	Words Without Long <u>o</u>
Words With <u>y</u>	**Words Without <u>y</u>**

SCHOOL-HOME CONNECTION Shuffle the Spelling
Word cards. Point to each one and have your child
read it to you. Talk about how the words are alike and
how they are different.

© Harcourt

Name _____

Practice Test

▶ Read each pair of sentences. Look at how the underlined words are spelled. Then fill in the oval next to the correct sentence.

SAMPLE: ⬤ Here comes a <u>bunny</u>.
○ Here comes a <u>bunnie</u>.

1. ○ He has such a furry <u>face</u>.
   ○ He has such a furry <u>fase</u>.

2. ○ His big <u>fete</u> are nice.
   ○ His big <u>feet</u> are nice.

3. ○ I want to <u>try</u> to hop like him.
   ○ I want to <u>trie</u> to hop like him.

4. ○ <u>How</u> does he make it look easy?
   ○ <u>Howe</u> does he make it look easy?

5. ○ He beat me to the <u>gaet</u>!
   ○ He beat me to the <u>gate</u>!

Practice Test

▶ Read each sentence. Look at how the two words are spelled. Fill in the oval next to the correct word.

SAMPLE: Jess _____ late to the picnic.

— came   ⬭ caem

1. She rode her _____ around the pond.
   ⬭ bik   ⬭ bike

2. _____ she rode, she saw many birds.
   ⬭ Wile   ⬭ While

3. She pedaled into a puddle and
   splashed in the _____.
   ⬭ woter   ⬭ water

4. _____ birds flew down to look.
   ⬭ Nine   ⬭ Nin

5. One of _____ birds followed Jess home.
   ⬭ thoze   ⬭ those

© Harcourt

Name _____

► Unscramble the letters to write a
Spelling Word.

1. gthil

_____
- - - - - - - - -
_____

2. oshet

_____
- - - - - - - - -
_____

3. tihgn

_____
- - - - - - - - -
_____

4. wevelt

_____
- - - - - - - - -
_____

5. irbgth

_____
- - - - - - - - -
_____

6. droe

_____
- - - - - - - - -
_____

7. ighh

_____
- - - - - - - - -
_____

8. cutho

_____
- - - - - - - - -
_____

9. ihmtg

_____
- - - - - - - - -
_____

10. gtrih

_____
- - - - - - - - -
_____

Spelling Words

high
night
light
right
might
bright
rode
those
touch
twelve

© Harcourt

SCHOOL-HOME CONNECTION Have your child read
each Spelling Word to you. Ask what letters stand for the
vowel sound in each word.

SPELLING PRACTICE BOOK
GATHER AROUND • LESSON 1
67

► Write the letter or letters that complete each Spelling Word. Then trace the rest of the word.

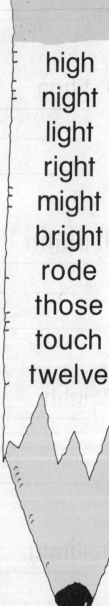

Spelling Words

high
night
light
right
might
bright
rode
those
touch
twelve

1. mi

2. tw

3. n t

4. tho

5. t ch

6. ri

7.

8. br

► Unscramble the letters to make a Spelling Word.

9. g h h i

10. e r o d

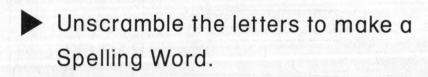

SCHOOL-HOME CONNECTION Write the words *tight, rope, these,* and *torch.* Have your child change one letter in each word to make a Spelling Word.

Word Sorts

► Make cards for the Spelling Words. Lay them down and read them.

1. Put the words with long <u>a</u> in one group and those without long <u>a</u> in another group. Write the words on the chart.

2. Put the words with long <u>i</u> in one group and those without long <u>i</u> in another group. Then write the words.

Words With Long <u>a</u>	Words Without Long <u>a</u>
Words With Long <u>i</u>	**Words Without Long <u>i</u>**

Spelling Words

day

say

sail

pail

pay

play

right

high

learn

join

My Own Word

SCHOOL-HOME CONNECTION Point to and read the Spelling Words aloud with your child. Talk about how the words are alike and how they are different.

SPELLING PRACTICE BOOK
GATHER AROUND • LESSON 2 69

© Harcourt

Name _____

▶ Write the letter or letters that complete each Spelling Word. Then trace the rest of the word.

Spelling Words

day
say
sail
pail
pay
play
right
high
learn
join

1. h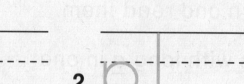

2. pl

3. 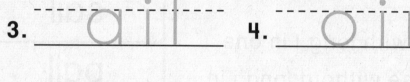ail

4. 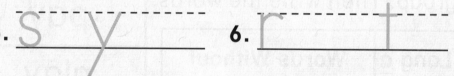oin

5. s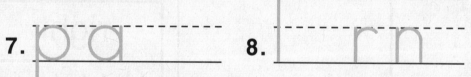y

6. r___t

7. pa___

8. ___rn

▶ Unscramble the letters to make a Spelling Word.

9. i l s a _____

10. a y d _____

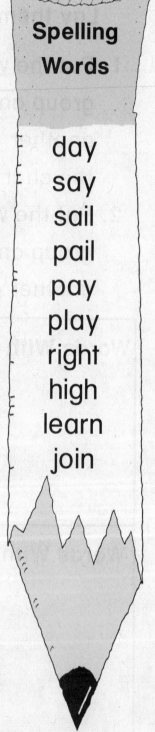

SCHOOL-HOME CONNECTION Write the words *may*, *clay*, *fight*, and *coin*. Have your child change one letter in each word to make a Spelling Word.

© Harcourt

Name _____

▶ Unscramble the letters to write a
   Spelling Word.

1. licdh

_____

- - - - - - - - - - - - - - - - -

_____

2. yapl

_____

- - - - - - - - - - - - - - - - -

_____

3. usre

_____

- - - - - - - - - - - - - - - - -

_____

4. fdni

_____

- - - - - - - - - - - - - - - - -

_____

5. dilm

_____

- - - - - - - - - - - - - - - - -

_____

6. nso

_____

- - - - - - - - - - - - - - - - -

_____

7. yda

_____

- - - - - - - - - - - - - - - - -

_____

8. nidm

_____

- - - - - - - - - - - - - - - - -

_____

9. inkd

_____

- - - - - - - - - - - - - - - - -

_____

10. idwl

_____

- - - - - - - - - - - - - - - - -

_____

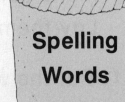

**Spelling
Words**

find
kind
mind
mild
child
wild
day
play
sure
son

© Harcourt

SCHOOL-HOME CONNECTION Have your child read
each Spelling Word to you. Tell him or her to make a
check mark next to all the words that have long *i* as in
bind.

Word Sorts

▶ Make cards for the Spelling Words. Lay them down and read them.

1. Put the words with long i in one group and those without long i in another group. Write the words on the chart.

2. Put the words with ay in one group and those without ay in another. Write the words on the chart.

Spelling Words

| find |
| kind |
| mind |
| mild |
| child |
| wild |
| day |
| play |
| sure |
| son |

My Own Word

Words With Long i	Words Without Long i
Words With ay	**Words Without ay**

SCHOOL-HOME CONNECTION Point to and read the Spelling Words aloud with your child. Talk about how the words are alike and how they are different.

© Harcourt

Word Sorts

▶ Make cards for the Spelling Words. Lay them down and read them.

1. Put the words with long <u>o</u> in one group and those without long <u>o</u> in another. Write the words on the chart.

2. Put the words with long <u>i</u> in one group and those without long <u>i</u> in another. Write the words on the chart.

Words With Long <u>o</u>	Words Without Long <u>o</u>
Words With Long <u>i</u>	**Words Without Long <u>i</u>**

Spelling Words

old
fold
told
cold
roll
most
find
child
both
during
My Own Word

SCHOOL-HOME CONNECTION Point to and read the Spelling Words aloud with your child. Talk about how the words are alike and how they are different.

SPELLING PRACTICE BOOK
GATHER AROUND • LESSON 4   73

Name _____

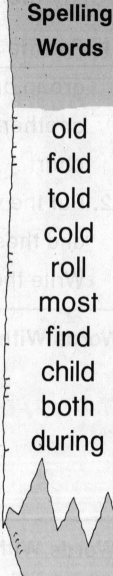

▶ Write the letter or letters that complete each Spelling Word. Then trace the rest of the word.

Spelling Words

old
fold
told
cold
roll
most
find
child
both
during

1.  co

2. 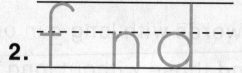 f nd

3. 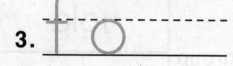 fo

4. 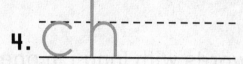 ch

5. 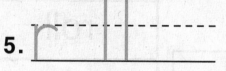 r ll

6.  dur

7. 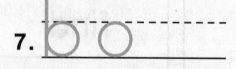 bo

8.  o

▶ Unscramble the letters to make a Spelling Word.

9. l d t o _____

10. o s m t _____

SCHOOL-HOME CONNECTION Write the words *hold*, *mind*, and *bath*. Have your child change one letter in each word to make a Spelling Word.

▶ Unscramble the letters to write a
Spelling Word.

1. rolfo

_____

- - - - - - - - - - - - -

_____

2. stom

_____

- - - - - - - - - - - - -

_____

3. peag

_____

- - - - - - - - - - - - -

_____

4. dufeg

_____

- - - - - - - - - - - - -

_____

5. dol

_____

- - - - - - - - - - - - -

_____

6. eag

_____

- - - - - - - - - - - - -

_____

7. icpee

_____

- - - - - - - - - - - - -

_____

8. dageb

_____

- - - - - - - - - - - - -

_____

9. geac

_____

- - - - - - - - - - - - -

_____

10. duebg

_____

- - - - - - - - - - - - -

_____

**Spelling
Words**

age
page
cage
badge
budge
fudge
old
most
floor
piece

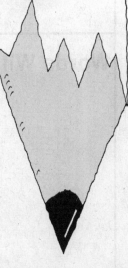

© Harcourt

SCHOOL-HOME CONNECTION Have your child read
each Spelling Word to you. Ask what he or she has
learned about the letter *g*.

Name _____

Word Sorts

▶ Make cards for the Spelling Words.
Lay them down and read them.

1. Put the words with <u>ge</u> in one group
and those without <u>ge</u> in another.
Write the words on the chart.

2. Put the words with long <u>a</u> in one
group and those without long <u>a</u> in
another. Write the words on the chart.

Spelling Words

age
page
cage
badge
budge
fudge
old
most
floor
piece
My Own Word

Words With <u>ge</u>	Words Without <u>ge</u>
Words With Long <u>a</u>	**Words Without Long <u>a</u>**

© Harcourt

SCHOOL-HOME CONNECTION Shuffle the Spelling
Word cards, then point to each one and read it aloud
with your child. Talk about how the words are alike
and how they are different.

Name _____

► Unscramble the letters to write a
Spelling Word.

1. beut

_____

- - - - - - - - - - - - - - - - - - - -

_____

2. sue

_____

- - - - - - - - - - - - - - - - - - - -

_____

3. epag

_____

- - - - - - - - - - - - - - - - - - - -

_____

4. rorys

_____

- - - - - - - - - - - - - - - - - - - -

_____

5. tecu

_____

- - - - - - - - - - - - - - - - - - - -

_____

6. edguf

_____

- - - - - - - - - - - - - - - - - - - -

_____

7. ubce

_____

- - - - - - - - - - - - - - - - - - - -

_____

8. ghue

_____

- - - - - - - - - - - - - - - - - - - -

_____

9. reul

_____

- - - - - - - - - - - - - - - - - - - -

_____

10. yargn

_____

- - - - - - - - - - - - - - - - - - - -

_____

**Spelling
Words**

tube
cube
cute
use
rule
huge
page
fudge
angry
sorry

© Harcourt

SCHOOL-HOME CONNECTION Have your child read
each Spelling Word to you. Ask which words have a long
vowel sound in the middle and a silent *e* at the end.

Name _____

► Write the letter or letters that complete each Spelling Word. Then trace the rest of the word.

Spelling Words

1. r l

2. cut

3. u e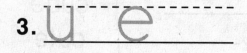

4. so

5. tu e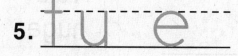

6. an

7. age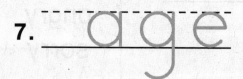

8. fu

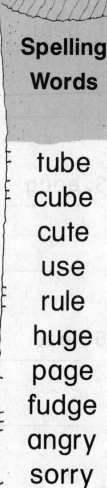
tube
cube
cute
use
rule
huge
page
fudge
angry
sorry

► Unscramble the letters to make a Spelling Word.

9. g u e h _____

10. b e u c _____

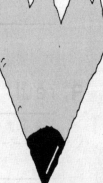

SCHOOL-HOME CONNECTION Write the words *tune, pave, rude,* and *judge.* Have your child change one letter in each word to make a Spelling Word.

© Harcourt

Word Sorts

► Make cards for the Spelling Words.
Lay them down and read them.

1. Put the words with <u>ea</u> in one group and those without <u>ea</u> in another. Write the words on the chart.

2. Put the words with long <u>u</u> in one group and those without long <u>u</u> in another. Write the words on the chart.

Words With <u>ea</u>	Words Without <u>ea</u>
Words With Long <u>u</u>	**Words Without Long <u>u</u>**

Spelling Words

lead
head
bread
read
ready
heavy
rule
use
few
boy
My Own Word

© Harcourt

SCHOOL-HOME CONNECTION Ask your child why he or she wrote the Spelling Words in each part of the chart.

SPELLING PRACTICE BOOK
GATHER AROUND • LESSON 7   79

Name _____

▶ Write the letter or letters that complete each Spelling Word. Then trace the rest of the word. Use each word only once.

Spelling Words

lead
head
bread
read
ready
heavy
rule
use
few
boy

1. _____ oy

2. br _____

3. _____ ad

4. _____ dy

5. _____ vy

6. f _____

7. h _____ d

8. u _____

9. r _____ d

10. ru _____

SCHOOL-HOME CONNECTION Write the words *lean*, *heat* and *toy*. Have your child change one letter in each word to make a Spelling Word.

© Harcourt

Name _____

▶ Unscramble the letters to write a
Spelling Word.

Spelling Words

1. toto
_____
_ _ _ _ _ _ _ _ _ _ _
_____

2. dear
_____
_ _ _ _ _ _ _ _ _ _ _
_____

3. hotob
_____
_ _ _ _ _ _ _ _ _ _ _
_____

4. raycr
_____
_ _ _ _ _ _ _ _ _ _ _
_____

5. loco
_____
_ _ _ _ _ _ _ _ _ _ _
_____

6. dhae
_____
_ _ _ _ _ _ _ _ _ _ _
_____

7. oolt
_____
_ _ _ _ _ _ _ _ _ _ _
_____

8. shuro
_____
_ _ _ _ _ _ _ _ _ _ _
_____

9. thoto
_____
_ _ _ _ _ _ _ _ _ _ _
_____

10. tboo
_____
_ _ _ _ _ _ _ _ _ _ _
_____

Spelling Words list:
cool
tool
toot
tooth
booth
boot
read
head
carry
hours

© Harcourt

SCHOOL-HOME CONNECTION Have your child read
each Spelling Word to you. Talk about the letters that
stand for the vowel sounds in the words.

Name _____

▶ Write the letter or letters that complete each Spelling Word. Then trace the rest of the words.

1.  c o o

2. 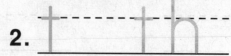 t_ th

3. 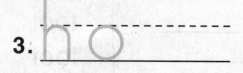 h o

4. 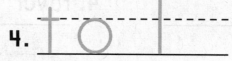 t o l

5.  t o t

6.  c a

7.  r e d

8.  b_ th

Spelling Words

cool
tool
toot
tooth
booth
boot
read
head
carry
hours

▶ Unscramble the letters to make a Spelling Word.

9. o t b o

_____

10. e h a d

_____

© Harcourt

SCHOOL-HOME CONNECTION Write the words *foot*, *bead*, *marry*, and *cook*. Have your child change one letter in each word to make a Spelling Word.

Practice Test

▶ Read each sentence. Look at how the two words are spelled. Fill in the oval next to the correct word.

SAMPLE: Most _____ birds are out in the daytime.
- ⬯ wiled   ⬛ wild

1. Some birds only come out at _____.
- ⬯ night   ⬯ nite

2. _____ night birds see in the dark.
- ⬯ Must   ⬯ Most

3. Lots of birds can fly _____ in the sky.
- ⬯ hie   ⬯ high

4. Do not try to put a wild bird in a _____.
- ⬯ cage   ⬯ caje

5. That would make the bird _____.
- ⬯ aingry   ⬯ angry

© Harcourt

Practice Test

▶ Read each pair of sentences. Look at how the underlined words are spelled. Then fill in the oval next to the correct sentence.

SAMPLE: ⬭ Jackson has <u>red</u> many books.

⬛ Jackson has <u>read</u> many books.

1. ⬭ Some of his books are big and <u>heavy</u>.

   ⬭ Some of his books are big and <u>hevy</u>.

2. ⬭ He knows he can <u>lern</u> a lot from them.

   ⬭ He knows he can <u>learn</u> a lot from them.

3. ⬭ He thinks it is fun to <u>finde</u> out new things.

   ⬭ He thinks it is fun to <u>find</u> out new things.

4. ⬭ Each <u>page</u> tells him more.

   ⬭ Each <u>paje</u> tells him more.

5. ⬭ Jackson never has to be <u>told</u> to read!

   ⬭ Jackson never has to be <u>tolde</u> to read!

Spelling Strategies

Look for word families...

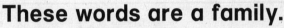

These words are a family.

- Words in a word family rhyme.
- The first letters are different.
- The other letters are the same.

> I want to spell ___.
> The letter **h** stands for the beginning sound.
> A word in the same family is **pen**.
> I'll add the letters **en** and write **hen**.

Word families can help you spell words.

- Think about the beginning sound of the word you want to spell.
- Write the letter that stands for this sound.
- Think of a word in the same word family.
- Write the letters that are the same.

Harcourt

Word Sort Cards

Write a Spelling Word in each box.

Cut out the word cards. Sort the words.

See how many ways you can sort the words.

Harcourt

Handwriting
Capital and Lowercase Manuscript Alphabet

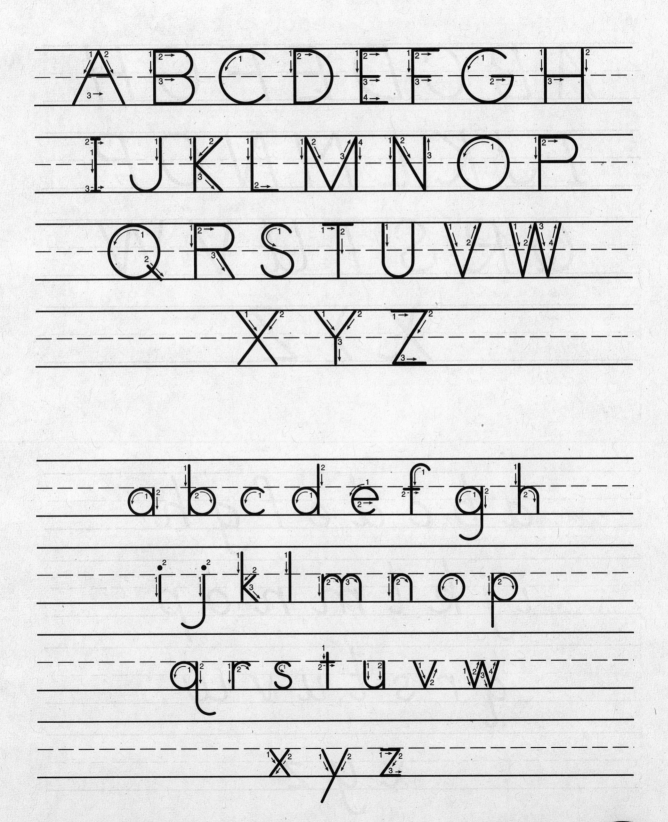

Handwriting

D'Nealian Capital and Lowercase Manuscript Alphabet

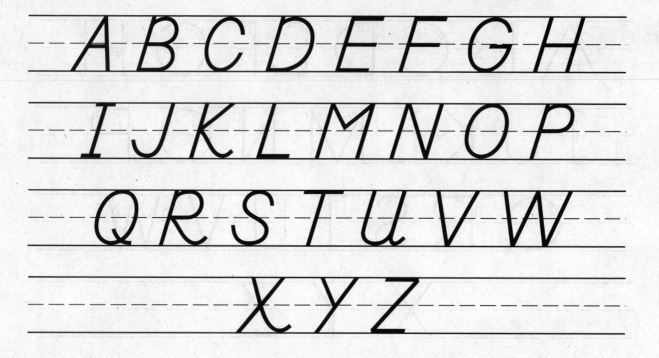

A B C D E F G H
I J K L M N O P
Q R S T U V W
X Y Z

a b c d e f g h
i j k l m n o p
q r s t u v w
x y z

Harcourt